THE AUTOBIOGRAPHY OF ST IGNATIUS

The Autobiography of St. Ignatius

Edited By
J. F. X. O'Conor, S.J.

CANA PRESS

Imprimatur.
Michael Augustine,
Archbishop of New York.
Nihil obstat.

Edwardus I. Purbrick, S.J.,
*Præpositus Provincialis Provinciæ
Marylandiæ Neo-Eboracensis.*

Jacobus J. Casey, S.J.,
Censor Deputatus.

New York, Dec. 14, 1899.

Originally published in 1900, by Benziger Brothers, New York, Cincinnati, Chicago.

Newly typeset and edited by Notre Dame Priory

Cana Press © 2024

All rights reserved.

No part of this book may be reproduced or transmitted, in any form or by any means, without permission.

For information, address:
PO Box 85,
Colebrook,
Tasmania, 7027,
Australia

notredamemonastery.org

ISBN
978-0-9756588-8-8

Editor's Preface

This account of the life of St. Ignatius, dictated by himself, is considered by the Bollandists the most valuable record of the great Founder of the Society of Jesus. The editors of the *Stimmen Aus Maria Laach*, the German review, as well as those of the English magazine, *The Month*, tell us that it, more than any other work, gives an insight into the spiritual life of St. Ignatius. Few works in ascetical literature, except the writings of St. Teresa and St. Augustine, impart such a knowledge of the soul. To understand fully the Spiritual Exercises, we should know something of the man who wrote them. In this life of St. Ignatius, told in his own words, we acquire an intimate knowledge of the author of the Exercises. We discern the Saint's natural disposition, which was the foundation of his spiritual character. We learn of his conversion, his trials, the obstacles in his way, the heroism with which he accomplished his great mission. This autobiography of St. Ignatius is the groundwork of all the great lives of him that have been written. Bartoli draws from it, Genelli develops it, the recent magnificent works of Father Clair, S.J., and of

Stewart Rose are amplifications of this simple story of the life of St. Ignatius. The Saint in his narrative always refers to himself in the third person, and this mode of speech has here been retained. Many persons who have neither the time, nor, perhaps, the inclination, to read larger works, will read, we trust, with pleasure and profit this autobiography. Ignatius, as he lay wounded in his brother's house, read the lives of the saints to while away the time. Touched by grace, he cried, "What St. Francis and St. Dominic have done, that, by God's grace, I will do." May this little book, in like manner, inspire its readers with the desire of imitating St. Ignatius.

The Editor.
Easter, 1900.
College of St. Francis Xavier,
New York.

Preface of the Writer

Preface of Father Louis Gonzalez, S.J., to the "Acts of St. Ignatius," received from the lips of the Saint and translated into Latin by Father Hannibal Codretto, S.J.

Jesus, Mary. In the year 1553, one Friday morning, August 4, the eve of the feast of Our Lady of the Snows, while St. Ignatius was in the garden, I began to give him an account of my soul, and, among other things, I spoke to him of how I was tempted by vain glory. The spiritual advice he gave me was this: "Refer everything that you do to God; strive to offer Him all the good you find in yourself, acknowledging that this comes from God, and thank Him for it." The advice given to me on this occasion was so consoling to me that I could not refrain from tears. St. Ignatius then related to me that for two years he had struggled against vain glory; so much so, indeed, that when he was about to embark for Jerusalem at Barcelona he did not dare to tell any one where he was going. He told me, moreover, that since that time his soul had experienced great peace in regard to this matter.

An hour or two later we went to dinner, and, while

Master Polancus and I were dining with him, St. Ignatius said that Master Natalis and others of the Society had often asked him to give a narrative of his life, but he had never as yet decided to do so. On this occasion, however, after I had spoken to him, he reflected upon it alone. He was favourably inclined toward it. From the way he spoke, it was evident God had enlightened him. He had resolved to manifest the main points of his interior life up to the present, and had concluded that I was the one to whom he would make these things known. At that time St. Ignatius was in very feeble health. He did not promise himself one day of life, but, on the contrary, if any one were to say, "I shall do that within two weeks or a week," St. Ignatius was accustomed to say: "How is that? Do you think you are going to live that long?" However, on this occasion, he said he hoped to live three or four months to finish the narrative.

The next day when I asked him when he wished to begin, he answered that I should remind him every day until he had an opportunity for it. As he could not find time, partly on account of his many occupations, he told me to remind him of it every Sunday. In the following September he called me, and began to relate his whole life clearly and distinctly with all the accompanying circumstances. Afterward, in the same month, he called me three or four times, and told me the history of his life up to the time of his dwelling at Manresa.

The method followed by St. Ignatius is so clear that he places vividly before our eyes the events of the past. It was not necessary to ask him anything, as nothing important was omitted. I began to write down certain points immediately, and I afterward filled out the details. I endeavoured to write nothing that I did not hear from him.

So closely did I adhere to his very words that afterward I was unable to explain the meaning of some of them. This narrative I wrote, as I have indicated above, up to September, 1553. From that time until the 18th of October, 1554, when Father Natalis came, St. Ignatius did not continue the narrative, but pleaded excuse on account of infirmities or other business, saying to me, "When such and such a business is settled, remind me of it." When that work was done, I recalled it to his memory. He replied, "Now I have that other affair on hand; when it is finished remind me."

Father Natalis was overjoyed that a beginning had been made, and told me to urge St. Ignatius to complete it, often saying to me, "In no other way can you do more good to the Society, for this is fundamentally the Society." He himself spoke to St. Ignatius about it, and I was told to remind him of it when the work in regard to the founding of the college was finished. And when it was over, and the business with Prester John settled and the courier had departed, we continued the history on the 9th of March, 1555. About this time Pope Julius became ill, and died on the 23d of the same month. The narrative was then postponed until the election of the new Pope, who died soon after his election.

Our work remained untouched until Pope Paul mounted the papal throne. On account of the great heat and many occupations, the biography did not make much progress until the 21st of September, when there was question of sending me to Spain. And so he appointed the morning of the 22d for a meeting in the red tower. After saying Mass I went to him to ask him if it were the time. He told me to go and wait for him in the red tower. Supposing that I should have to wait a long while, I delayed on the porch, talking with a brother who asked me about something. When St. Ignatius came he reprimanded me because, contrary to obedience, I had not waited for him in the appointed place, and he would not do anything that day. Then we urged him very earnestly to continue. So he came to the red tower, and, according to his custom, dictated while walking. While taking these notes I tried to see his face, and kept drawing near to him. He said to me, "Keep your rule." And as I approached again, and looked at him a second and a third time, he repeated what he had said and then went away. Finally, after some time, he returned to the red tower to complete the dictation. As I was about starting on my journey, and St. Ignatius spoke to me the day before my departure, I could not write out the narrative in full at Rome. At Genoa where I went I had no Spanish secretary, so I dictated in Latin the points I had brought with me, and finished the writing at Genoa in December, 1555.

Contents

Editor's Preface v

Preface of the Writer vii

CHAPTER I 1
HIS MILITARY LIFE—HE IS WOUNDED AT THE SIEGE OF PAMPELUNA—HIS CURE—SPIRITUAL READING—THE APPARITION—THE GIFT OF CHASTITY—HIS LONGING FOR THE JOURNEY TO JERUSALEM AND FOR A HOLIER LIFE

CHAPTER II 6
IGNATIUS LEAVES HIS NATIVE LAND—WHAT HE DID AT MONTSERRAT AND AT MANRESA

CHAPTER III 14
SCRUPLES—HEAVENLY FAVORS—JOURNEY TO BARCELONA

CHAPTER IV 22
HIS JOURNEY TO ROME, VENICE, JERUSALEM, AND THE HOLY LAND

CHAPTER V 27
HIS ARRIVAL IN APULIA, VENICE, FERRARA, AND GENOA—HE IS APPREHENDED AS A SPY—HE IS DESPISED AS A FOOL—HIS STUDIES AT BARCELONA AND ALCALA

CHAPTER VI 34
THE PRISONS AT ALCALA AND SALAMANCA

CHAPTER VII 42
HIS STUDIES IN PARIS, AND OTHER INCIDENTS OF HIS LIFE

CHAPTER VIII 50
HIS ARRIVAL IN HIS NATIVE LAND AND THE VIRTUES PRACTISED THERE—HIS JOURNEY INTO SPAIN AND ITALY—THE FAMOUS APPARITION AND HIS LIFE IN THE SAME PLACE

APPENDIX 57

CHAPTER I

HIS MILITARY LIFE—HE IS WOUNDED AT THE SIEGE OF PAMPLONA—HIS CURE—SPIRITUAL READING—THE APPARITION—THE GIFT OF CHASTITY—HIS LONGING FOR THE JOURNEY TO JERUSALEM AND FOR A HOLIER LIFE

Up to his twenty-sixth year the heart of Ignatius was enthralled by the vanities of the world. His special delight was in the military life, and he seemed led by a strong and empty desire of gaining for himself a great name. The citadel of Pamplona was held in siege by the French. All the other soldiers were unanimous in wishing to surrender on condition of freedom to leave, since it was impossible to hold out any longer; but Ignatius so persuaded the commander, that, against the views of all the other nobles, he decided to hold the citadel against the enemy.

When the day of assault came, Ignatius made his confession to one of the nobles, his companion in arms. The soldier also made his to Ignatius. After the walls were destroyed, Ignatius stood fighting bravely until a cannon ball of the enemy broke one of his legs and seriously injured the other.

When he fell, the citadel was surrendered. When the French took possession of the town, they showed great admiration for Ignatius. After twelve or fifteen days at Pamplona, where he received the best care from the physicians of the French army, he was borne on a litter to Loyola. His recovery was very slow, and doctors and surgeons were summoned from all parts for a consultation. They decided that the leg should be broken again, that the bones, which had knit badly, might be properly reset; for they had not been properly set in the beginning, or else had been so jostled on the journey that a cure was impossible. He submitted to have his flesh cut again. During the operation, as in all he suffered before and after, he uttered no word and gave no sign of suffering save that of tightly clenching his fists.

In the meantime his strength was failing. He could take no food, and showed other symptoms of approaching death. On the feast of St John the doctors gave up hope of his recovery, and he was advised to make his confession. Having received the sacraments on the eve of the feasts of Ss Peter and Paul, toward evening the doctors said that if by the middle of the night there were no change for the better, he would surely die. He had great devotion to St Peter, and it so happened by the goodness of God that in the middle of the night he began to grow better.

His recovery was so rapid that in a few days he was out of danger. As the bones of his leg settled and pressed upon each other, one bone protruded below the knee. The result was that one leg was shorter than the other, and the bone causing a lump there, made the leg seem quite deformed. As he could not bear this, since he intended to live a life at court, he asked the doctors whether the bone could be cut away. They replied that it could, but it would cause him more suffering than all that had preceded, as everything was healed, and they would need space in order to cut it. He determined, however, to undergo this torture.

His elder brother looked on with astonishment and admiration. He said he could never have had the fortitude to suffer the pain which the sick man bore with his usual patience. When the flesh and the bone that protruded were cut away, means were taken to prevent the leg from becoming shorter than the other. For this purpose, in spite of sharp and constant pain, the leg was kept stretched for many days. Finally the Lord gave him health. He came out of the danger safe and strong with the exception that he could not easily stand on his leg, but was forced to lie in bed.

As Ignatius had a love for fiction, when he found himself out of danger he asked for some romances to pass away the time. In that house there was no book of the kind. They gave him, instead, *The Life of Christ*, by Rudolph, the Carthusian, and another book called the *Flowers of the Saints*, both in Spanish. By frequent reading of these books he began to get some love for spiritual things. This reading led his mind to meditate on holy things, yet sometimes it wandered to thoughts which he had been accustomed to dwell upon before.

Among these there was one thought which, above the others, so filled his heart that he became, as it were, immersed and absorbed in it. Unconsciously, it engaged his attention for three and four hours at a time. He pictured to himself what he should do in honour of an illustrious lady, how he should journey to the city where she was, in what words he would address her, and what bright and pleasant sayings he would make use of, what manner of warlike exploits he should perform to please her. He was so carried away by this thought that he did not even perceive how far beyond his power it was to do what he proposed, for she was a lady exceedingly illustrious and of the highest nobility.

In the meantime the divine mercy was at work substituting for these thoughts others suggested by his recent readings. While perusing the life of Our Lord and the saints, he began to reflect, saying to himself: 'What if I should do what St Francis did?' 'What if I should act like St Dominic?' He pondered over these things in his mind, and kept continually proposing to himself serious and difficult things. He seemed to feel a certain readiness for doing them, with no other reason except this thought: 'St Dominic did this; I, too, will do it.' 'St Francis did this; therefore I will do it.' These heroic resolutions remained for a time, and then other vain and worldly thoughts followed. This succession of thoughts occupied him for a long while, those about God alternating with those about the world. But in these thoughts there was this difference. When he thought of worldly things it gave him great pleasure, but afterward he found himself dry and sad. But when he thought of journeying to Jerusalem, and of living only on herbs, and practising austerities, he found pleasure not only while thinking of them, but also when he had ceased.

This difference he did not notice or value, until one day the eyes of his soul were opened and he began to inquire the reason of the difference. He learned by experience that one train of thought left him sad, the other joyful. This was his first reasoning on spiritual matters. Afterward, when he began the Spiritual Exercises, he was enlightened, and understood what he afterward taught his children about the discernment of spirits. When gradually he recognised the different spirits by which he was moved, one, the spirit of God, the other, the devil, and when he had gained no little spiritual light from the reading of pious books, he began to think more seriously of his past life, and how much penance he should do to expiate his past sins.

Amid these thoughts the holy wish to imitate saintly men came to his mind; his resolve was not more definite than to promise with the help of divine grace that what they had done he also would do. After his recovery his one wish was to make a pilgrimage to Jerusalem. He fasted frequently and scourged himself to satisfy the desire of penance that ruled in a soul filled with the spirit of God.

The vain thoughts were gradually lessened by means of these desires—desires that were not a little strengthened by the following vision. While watching one night he plainly saw the image of the Blessed Mother of God with the Infant Jesus, at the sight of which, for a considerable time, he received abundant consolation, and felt such contrition for his past life that he thought of nothing else. From that time until August, 1555, when this was written, he never felt the least motion of concupiscence. This privilege we may suppose from this fact to have been a divine gift, although we dare not state it, nor say anything except confirm what has been already said. His brother and all in the house recognised from what appeared externally how great a change had taken place in his soul.

He continued his reading meanwhile, and kept the holy resolution he had made. At home his conversation was wholly devoted to divine things, and helped much to the spiritual advancement of others.

CHAPTER II

IGNATIUS LEAVES HIS NATIVE LAND—WHAT HE DID AT MONT-SERRAT AND AT MANRESA

Ignatius, starting from his father's house, set out upon his journey on horseback. About this time he began his habit of taking the discipline every night. His brother desired to accompany him as far as Ogna, and during the journey was persuaded by the Saint to pass one night of watching at the shrine of Our Blessed Lady at Aruncuz. Having prayed some time at the shrine for new strength for his journey, leaving his brother at Ogna at the house of their sister, to whom he paid a short visit, he journeyed on to Navarre. Remembering that an official in the Duke's palace owed him some money, he collected it by sending in a written account to the treasurer, and distributed it among persons to whom he felt indebted. A portion of the money he devoted to the restoration of a picture of the Blessed Virgin. Then dismissing his two remaining servants, he rode forth alone from Navarre in the direction of Montserrat, a mountain town of Catalonia in the northern part of Spain.

It will not be amiss to recall an event that occurred during this journey, to show the manner in which God directed him. Although filled with an ardent desire of serving God, yet his knowledge of spiritual things was still very obscure. He had undertaken to perform extraordinary penances, not so much with a view to satisfy for his sins as with the intention of doing something pleasing to his Lord. He declared indeed that though filled with the liveliest abhorrence of his past sins, he could not assure himself that they were forgiven; yet in his austerities so intense was his desire to do great things for Christ that he did not think of his sins. When he recalled the penances practised by holy persons, his whole mind was bent on doing something to equal and even surpass them. In this holy ambition he found his consolation, for he had no interior motive for his penances, knowing as yet very little about humility or charity or patience, for to obtain these many holy men have led austere lives. He knew still less the value of discretion, which regulates the practice of these virtues. To do something great for the glory of his God, to emulate saintly men in all that they had done before him — this was the only object of Ignatius in his practices of external mortification.

While he journeyed on, a Saracen mounted on a horse came up with him. In the course of the conversation mention was made of the Blessed Virgin. The stranger remarked that though he admitted that the Mother of Christ had conceived without detriment to her virginal purity, yet he could not believe that after the conception of her divine Son she was still a virgin. He was so obstinate in holding this opinion, that no amount of reasoning on the part of Ignatius could force him to abandon it. Shortly afterward the Saracen rode on, leaving the pilgrim to his own reflections. These were not of the most peaceful nature. He was sorely troubled as he thought over the conduct of his recent fellow-traveller, and felt that he had but poorly acquitted himself of his duty of honouring the Mother of God. The longer his mind thought upon the matter, the more his soul was filled with indignation against himself for having allowed the Saracen to speak as he had done of the Blessed Virgin, and for the lack of courage he fancied he had shown in not at once resenting the insult. He consequently felt impelled by a strong impulse to hasten after him and slay the miscreant for the insulting language he had used. After much internal conflict with these thoughts, he still remained in doubt, nor could he decide what course to follow. The Saracen, who had ridden on, had mentioned to him that it was his intention to proceed to a town not far distant from the high road. At length, Ignatius, wearied by his inward struggle and not arriving at any determination, decided to settle all his doubts in the following novel way: he would give free rein to his horse, and if, on coming to the cross-road, his horse should turn into the path that led to the destination of the Moor, he would pursue him and kill him; but if his horse kept to the high road he would allow the wretch to escape. Having done as he had decided, it happened through the Providence of God that his horse kept to the high road, though the place was distant only about thirty or forty yards, and the way leading to it was very wide and easy.

Arriving at a large village situated a short distance from Montserrat, he determined to procure a garment to wear on his journey to Jerusalem. He therefore bought a piece of sackcloth, poorly woven, and filled with prickly wooden fibres. Of this he made a garment that reached to his feet. He bought, also, a pair of shoes of coarse stuff that is often used in making brooms. He never wore but one shoe, and that not for the sake of the comfort to be derived from it, but because, as he was in the habit of wearing a cord tied below the knee by way of mortification, this leg would be very much swollen at night, though he rode all day on horseback. For this reason, he felt he ought to wear a shoe on that foot. He provided himself also with a pilgrim's staff and a gourd to drink from. All these he tied to his saddle.

Thus equipped, he continued on his way to Montserrat, pondering in his mind, as was his wont, on the great things he would do for the love of God. And as he had formerly read the stories of Amadeus of Gaul and other such writers, who told how the Christian knights of the past were accustomed to spend the entire night, preceding the day on which they were to receive knighthood, on guard before an altar of the Blessed Virgin, he was filled with these chivalric fancies, and resolved to prepare himself for a noble knighthood by passing a night in vigil before an altar of Our Lady at Montserrat. He would observe all the formalities of this ceremony, neither sitting nor lying down, but alternately standing and kneeling, and there he would lay aside his worldly dignities to assume the arms of Christ.

When he arrived at Montserrat, he passed a long time in prayer, and with the consent of his confessor he made in writing a general confession of his sins. Three whole days were employed in this undertaking. He begged and obtained leave of his confessor to give up his horse, and to hang up his sword and his dagger in the church, near the altar of the Blessed Virgin. This confessor was the first to whom he unfolded his interior, and disclosed his resolution of devoting himself to a spiritual life. Never before had he manifested his purpose to anybody.

The eve of the Annunciation of Our Blessed Lady in the year 1522 was the time he chose to carry out the project he had formed. At nightfall, unobserved by any one, he approached a beggar, and taking off his own costly garments gave them to the beggar. He then put on the pilgrim's dress he had previously bought, and hastened to the church, where he threw himself on his knees before the altar of the Blessed Mother of God, and there, now kneeling, now standing, with staff in hand, he passed the entire night.

After receiving the Blessed Sacrament, to avoid recognition he left the town at daybreak. He did not go by the direct route that leads to Barcelona, as he might have met those who knew him and would honour him, but he took a byway that led him to a town called Manresa. Here he determined to remain a few days in the hospital and write out some notes in his little book, which for his own consolation he carefully carried about with him. At about a league's distance from Montserrat, he was overtaken by a man who had ridden after him at a rapid pace. This man accosted him and inquired if he had given certain garments to a poor man, as the latter had declared. Ignatius answered that it was true that he had given them to a beggar. On learning that the latter had been ill-treated because he was suspected of having stolen the clothes, the eyes of Ignatius filled with tears, in pity for the poor man.

Although he had fled so anxiously from the praise of men, he did not remain long at Manresa before many marvellous things were narrated of him. This fame arose from what had occurred at Montserrat. His reputation increased day by day. Men vied with each other in adding some particulars about his sanctity, declaring that he had abandoned immense revenues, and other wonderful things without much regard to real facts.

At Manresa he lived on the alms that he daily begged. He never ate meat nor partook of wine, though they were offered him. On Sundays, however, he never fasted, and if wine were offered him, he drank of it sparingly. In former days he had been very careful of his hair, which he had worn, and, indeed, not unbecomingly, in the fashionable manner of the young men of his age; but now he determined to cease to care for it, neither to comb it nor to cut it, and to dispense with all covering for his head both day and night. To punish himself for the too great nicety which he had formerly had in the care of his hands and feet, he now resolved to neglect them.

It was while he was living at the hospital at Manresa that the following strange event took place. Very frequently on a clear moonlight night there appeared in the courtyard before him an indistinct shape which he could not see clearly enough to tell what it was. Yet it appeared so symmetrical and beautiful that his soul was filled with pleasure and joy as he gazed at it. It had something of the form of a serpent with glittering eyes, and yet they were not eyes. He felt an indescribable joy steal over him at the sight of this object. The oftener he saw it, the greater was the consolation he derived from it, and when the vision left him, his soul was filled with sorrow and sadness.

Up to this period he had remained in a constant state of tranquillity and consolation, without any interior knowledge of the trials that beset the spiritual life. But during the time that the vision lasted, sometimes for days, or a little previous to that time, his soul was violently agitated by a thought that brought him no little uneasiness. There flashed upon his mind the idea of the difficulty that attended the kind of life he had begun, and he felt as if he heard some one whispering to him, 'How can you keep up for seventy years of your life these practices which you have begun?' Knowing that this thought was a temptation of the evil one, he expelled it by this answer: 'Can you, wretched one, promise me one hour of life?' In this manner he overcame the temptation, and his soul was restored to peace. This was his first trial besides what has already been narrated, and it came upon him suddenly one day as he was entering the church. He was accustomed to hear Mass daily, and to assist at Vespers and Compline—devotions from which he derived much consolation. During Mass, he always read over the history of the Passion, and his soul was filled with a joyful feeling of uninterrupted calm.

Shortly after the temptation just spoken of, he began to experience great changes in his soul. At one time he was deprived of all consolation, so that he found no pleasure in vocal prayer, in hearing Mass, or in any spiritual exercise. At another, on the contrary, he suddenly felt as if all sorrow and desolation were taken from him, experiencing the relief of one from whose shoulders a heavy cloak had suddenly been lifted. On noticing all this, he was surprised, wondering what could be the import of these changes which he had never before experienced, and he said to himself, 'What new kind of life is this upon which I am entering?'

At this time he became acquainted with some holy persons who manifested great confidence in him, and gladly conversed with him; for though he had, as yet, little knowledge of spiritual things, still he spoke with great fervour on religious subjects, and incited his hearers to make greater progress in the way of God's service. Among those holy persons who dwelt at Manresa, there was one lady well advanced in years who had long been given to the service of God, and who was so well known in many places in Spain that his Catholic Majesty, the King of Spain, had desired her presence on one occasion in order to take counsel with her about certain projects that he had in his mind. This lady, speaking one day to our new soldier of Christ, said to him, 'Would that the Lord Jesus might appear to you some day!' Ignatius, wondering at her words, understood in a literal sense, and asked her, 'What would He look like if He were to show Himself to me?'

He always persevered in his custom of approaching the Sacraments of Confession and Holy Communion every week. But herein he found a great source of anxiety on account of the scruples with which he was annoyed. For though he had written out his general confession at Montserrat, and with great diligence and care had tried to make it complete, yet he always felt that he had forgotten something in his confession, and this caused him much anxiety. Even though he should now confess it again, he received no consolation. He tried then to find a spiritual person, who could give him relief in his trouble, but he found no one. Finally, a certain doctor who had experience in spiritual things, and who was a preacher in the church, advised him to write down anything he remembered and feared that he had not confessed. He obeyed, and even after he had confessed these sins, his scruples still continued to fill his soul, and he was constantly recalling minor details that he had not confessed. In this way he was cruelly tormented. He knew well that these scruples caused no little harm to the spiritual life, and that it was most expedient to get rid of them, yet they continued to torture him. At times it occurred to him that it would be well if he could have his confessor command him in the name of the Lord Jesus not again to confess anything of his past sins; and he inwardly prayed that his confessor would give him some such command, but he could not bring himself to ask him to do so.

CHAPTER III

SCRUPLES—HEAVENLY FAVOURS—JOURNEY TO BARCELONA

At last his confessor, without any suggestion on the part of the penitent, commanded him to confess nothing of his past life, except what was very clear and evident. But as he regarded everything of the past as evident, the confessor's order did not help him at all. He was in constant anxiety. At that time he lived in the Dominican monastery, in a little cell which the Fathers had allotted to him. He kept up his usual custom of praying on bended knees for seven hours a day, and scourged himself three times a day and during the night. But all this did not remove his scruples, which had been tormenting him for months. One day, when terribly tormented, he began to pray. During his prayer, he cried out to God in a loud voice: 'O Lord, help me, for I find no remedy among men, nor in any creature! If I thought I could find one, no labour would seem too great to me. Show me some one! O Lord! Where may I find one? I am willing to do anything to find relief.'

While tortured by these thoughts, several times he was violently tempted to cast himself out of the large window of his cell. This window was quite near the place where he was praying. But since he knew that it would be a sin to take his own life, he began to pray, 'O Lord, I will not do anything to offend Thee.' He repeated these words frequently with his former prayer, when there came to his mind the story of a certain holy man, who, to obtain of God some favour which he ardently desired, spent many days without food, until he obtained the favour he asked. He determined to do the same. He resolved in his heart neither to eat nor drink until God should look upon him in mercy, or until he should find himself at the point of death; then only should he eat.

This resolution was taken on a Sunday after communion, and for a whole week he neither ate nor drank anything; in the meantime he practised his usual penances, recited the Divine Office, prayed on bended knees at the appointed times, and rose at midnight. On the following Sunday, when about to make his usual confession, as he had been in the habit of making known to his confessor everything he had done, even the smallest detail, he told him that he had not eaten anything during the past week. Hereupon his confessor bade him break his fast. Although he felt that he still had sufficient strength to continue without food, nevertheless he obeyed his confessor, and on that day and the next he was free from scruples. On the third day, however, which was Tuesday, while standing in prayer, the remembrance of his sins came back to him. One suggested another, until he passed in review, one after another, all his past sins. He then thought he ought to repeat his general confession. After these thoughts a sort of disgust seized him, so that he felt an inclination to give up the life he was leading. While in this state, God was pleased to arouse him as it were from sleep, and to relieve him of his trouble. As he had acquired some experience in the discernment of spirits, he profited by the lessons he had learned of God, and began to examine how that spirit had entered into possession of his soul; then he resolved never again to speak of his past sins in confession. From that day he was free from scruples, and felt certain that it was the will of our merciful Lord to deliver him from his trouble of soul.

Besides the seven hours devoted to prayer, he spent a portion of his time in assisting souls who came to him for advice. During the rest of the day he gave his thoughts to God, pondering on what he had read or meditated that day. When he retired, it often happened that wonderful illuminations and great spiritual consolations came to him, so that he abridged the short time he had already allotted to sleep. Once while thinking over this matter he concluded that he had given sufficient time for conversation with God, and that moreover the whole day was also given to Him. Then he began to doubt whether these illuminations were from the Good Spirit. Finally he came to the conclusion that it would be better to give up a portion and to give sufficient time to sleep. This he did.

While he persevered in his resolution to abstain from meat, it happened on a certain morning after rising, that a dish of cooked meat seemed to be set before him. He appeared to see it with his eyes, although he had felt no previous craving for it. At the same time he afterward experienced within himself a certain movement of the will, urging him to eat meat. Although the remembrance of his former resolution came to mind, he had no doubt about determining to eat meat. When he made this known to his confessor, the latter advised him to consider whether it was a temptation or not. Pondering over it, he felt certain that he was right. At that period God dealt with him as a teacher instructing a pupil. Was this on account of his ignorance or dullness, or because he had no one else to teach him? Or on account of the fixed resolve he had of serving God, with which God Himself had inspired him, for the light given him could not possibly be greater? He was firmly convinced, both then and afterward, that God had treated him thus because it was the better spiritual training for him. The five following points will prove what he says:—

In the first place, he had a great devotion to the Blessed Trinity. Every day he prayed to each of the three Persons and to the whole Trinity. While thus praying to the Blessed Trinity, the thought came of how to offer fourfold prayers to the Divinity. This thought, however, caused him little or no trouble. Once, while reciting on the steps of the monastery the little hours in honour of the Blessed Virgin, his vision carried him beyond the earth. He seemed to behold the Blessed Trinity in the form of a lyre or harp; this vision affected him so much that he could not refrain from tears and sighs. On the same day he accompanied the procession from the church, but even up to the time of dinner he could not withhold his tears, and after dinner his joy and consolation were so great that he could speak of no subject except the Blessed Trinity. In these conversations he made use of many different comparisons to illustrate his thoughts. Such an impression was made on him on that occasion that during his after life, whenever he prayed to the Blessed Trinity, he experienced great devotion.

At another time, to his great joy, God permitted him to understand how He had created this world. This vision presented to him a white object, with rays emanating from it. From this object God sent forth light. However, he could not clearly explain this vision, nor could he recall the illuminations given to him by God on that occasion. During his stay of about a year at Manresa, after he had begun to receive from God consolations, and fruitful lights for the direction of others, he gave up his former rigorous penances. At that time he trimmed his nails and hair. During the time of his residence at Manresa, while assisting at Mass, he had another vision in the church of the monastery. At the elevation of the body of Christ Our Lord he beheld, with the eyes of his soul, white rays descending from above. Although he cannot, after so long an interval, explain the details of this vision, still the manner in which Our Lord Jesus Christ is present in the Blessed Sacrament was clearly and vividly stamped upon his mind. Often in prayer, and even during a long space of time, did he see the humanity of Christ with the eyes of the soul. The form under which this vision appeared was that of a white body, neither large nor small; besides, there seemed to be no distinction of members in His body. This vision appeared to him often at Manresa, perhaps twenty or even forty times, once at Jerusalem, and once when he was at Padua. He saw the Blessed Virgin under the same form, without any distinction of members. These visions gave him such strength that he often thought within himself, that even though Scripture did not bear witness to these mysteries of faith, still, from what he had seen, it would be his duty to lay down his life for them.

One day he went to the Church of St Paul, situated about a mile from Manresa. Near the road is a stream, on the bank of which he sat, and gazed at the deep waters flowing by. While seated there, the eyes of his soul were opened. He did not have any special vision, but his mind was enlightened on many subjects, spiritual and intellectual. So clear was this knowledge that from that day everything appeared to him in a new light. Such was the abundance of this light in his mind that all the divine helps received, and all the knowledge acquired up to his sixty-second year, were not equal to it.

From that day he seemed to be quite another man, and possessed of a new intellect. This illumination lasted a long time. While kneeling in thanksgiving for this grace, there appeared to him that object which he had often seen before, but had never understood. It seemed to be something most beautiful, and, as it were, gleaming with many eyes. This is how it always appeared. There was a cross near which he was praying, and he noticed that near the cross the vision had lost some of its former beautiful colour. He understood from this that the apparition was the work of the devil, and whenever the vision appeared to him after that, as it did several times, he dispelled it with his staff.

During a violent fever at Manresa, he thought he was near his death. The thought then came to his mind that he was already justified before God. Calling to mind his sins, he tried to combat the thought, but could not overcome it, and this struggle to overcome the temptation caused him much more suffering than the fever itself. After the fever had somewhat abated, and he was out of danger, he cried out to some noble ladies who had come to visit him, and asked them for the love of God, to cry out aloud the next time they should find him near death, 'O sinner!' and 'Remember the sins by which you have offended God.'

On another occasion, while sailing from Valencia to Italy, in the midst of a violent storm, the rudder was broken, and he and every one on board were convinced that the ship must founder unless help came from above. Then, as he examined his conscience and prepared for death, he had no dread on account of past sins, nor fear of eternal punishment, but he experienced intense shame and sorrow at the thought of not having made a good use of the favours and graces which God had bestowed upon him. Again, in the year 1550, he was dangerously ill, and in his own judgment and that of others he was about to die. This time, however, whenever he thought of death, such consolation poured into his soul that he wept tears of joy. He continued in this state so long that he often had to divert his mind from the thought of death, lest he should find in the thought too much consolation.

In the beginning of another winter he became very ill, and was placed under the care of the father of a man named Ferrera, who afterward entered the service of Balthasar Faria. Here he was very carefully attended. Several ladies of the highest rank were very devoted to him, and came every night to watch beside him. When he began to recover, he was still extremely weak, and suffered from severe pains in the stomach. These two causes, together with the intense cold and the entreaties of his attendants, induced him to wear shoes, warmer clothing, and a cap. He was obliged to accept two small coats of coarse greyish stuff, and a small cap of the same colour. During that illness his constant wish was to speak of spiritual things, and to find someone who could talk upon such subjects. Meanwhile the time which he had determined upon for his journey to Jerusalem was approaching.

In the beginning of the year 1523, therefore, he set out for Barcelona. Many offered to accompany him, but he refused, as he wished to go alone. He expected to derive great advantage from placing his whole trust in God alone. Several were very earnest, and insisted that as he knew neither Latin nor Italian, he should not go alone, but should take with him a certain companion whom they praised very much. Ignatius replied that even were he the son or brother of the Duke of Cordova, he would not take him as a companion, as he wished only three virtues,—Faith, Hope, and Charity. If he took a companion, when hungry he would look to his companion for food; if exhausted, he would call on his companion for help; and so he would confide in his companion, and have some affection for him: whereas he wished to place all this confidence, hope, and affection in God alone. These words were not a mere expression of the lips, but they were the true sentiments of his heart. For these reasons he wished to embark not only alone, but even without any provision for the voyage. When he arranged about his passage, the captain agreed to take him free, as he had no money; but on condition that he should take with him as much sailors' bread as would suffice for his sustenance. Were it not for this condition imposed by the captain, Ignatius would have refused to take with him any provision at all.

When he thought of procuring bread, he was much troubled with scruples. 'Is this your hope and faith in God, who, you were sure, would not fail you?' The force and violence of the temptation were such that he was greatly distressed. Good reasons on both sides presented themselves. Finally, in his perplexity, he determined to leave the matter to his confessor. He told him first of his great desire to go to Jerusalem, and to do everything for the greater glory of

God. Then he gave the reasons for not taking provisions for the voyage. His confessor decided that he ought to beg what was necessary and take it with him. He went to a lady of rank to ask for what he needed. When she asked where he was going, he hesitated a little about telling his final destination, and replied that he was going to Italy and Rome. She was somewhat astonished at this, and replied: 'To Rome? Why, as to those who go there—well, I do not like to say what they are when they return.' She meant by this that as most of those who went to Rome did not go through motives of piety and devotion, when they returned they were not much better. The reason of his not openly declaring that he intended to go to the holy city of Jerusalem was his dread of yielding to vainglory. In fact, he was so much troubled by this fear that he was afraid to make known even the place of his birth or the name of his family. When he had secured the bread, before going on board he took care to leave behind him, on a bench on the wharf, five or six Spanish coins, which had been given to him as alms.

He was obliged to remain at Barcelona more than twenty days before the ship was ready to sail. During that time, in accordance with his custom, in order to speak with spiritual men about his soul, he sought them out even though dwelling in hermitages at a long distance from the city. But neither then, nor during the whole time of his stay at Manresa, could he find anyone who could help him to advance as he wished. He met one woman, however, who seemed to be thoroughly acquainted with the spiritual life. She promised to pray to Jesus Christ and to ask Him to appear to Ignatius in person. In consequence of this promise, after leaving Barcelona, he gave up all anxiety about finding souls advanced in the spiritual life.

CHAPTER IV

HIS JOURNEY TO ROME, VENICE, JERUSALEM,
AND THE HOLY LAND

After a voyage of five days and nights the vessel in which they set out from Barcelona reached Gaeta, and the pilgrim disembarked and started for Rome, although there was danger there on account of the plague. After reaching the city, he found the gates closed. He spent the night in a damp church, and in the morning sought to enter the city, but could not obtain permission. As no alms could be obtained outside of the city, he wished to go on to a neighbouring village, but for sheer weakness, the pilgrim could go no farther. On that day it happened that a great procession came out of the city. On inquiry the pilgrim learned that the Duchess was in the throng. He approached her, told her that his malady was simply the effect of weakness, and asked permission to enter the city to get relief. She readily consented. He was successful and his strength returned, and two days later he resumed his journey, reaching Rome on Palm Sunday.

Those whom he met at Rome knew he had no money for his journey to Jerusalem. They tried to dissuade him from his undertaking, alleging that such a journey was impossible without money. He felt assured, however, that everything needed for his voyage would be at hand when required. Accordingly, on the octave of Easter, he received the blessing of Adrian VI and left Rome for Venice. He had in his possession six or seven pieces of gold which they had given him to pay his passage from Venice as far as Jerusalem. He had taken this money with him from Venice only because they had convinced him that without it he could not reach Jerusalem. On the third day from the time he set out from Rome, he realised that this fear had come from a want of confidence, and was sorry he had accepted the money, and was deliberating about giving it away. Finally, however, he determined to spend it on those he met, who were chiefly beggars. The result was that when he came to Venice he had only four coins left, and these were necessary for his lodging that night.

On this journey to Venice, on account of sentinels placed around the cities, he was obliged to sleep outside the walls. The dread of the pestilence was so great that one morning on rising he saw a man fleeing from him in terror. Pursuing his journey, he reached Chizoa with several others who had joined him on the road. There he learned that he would not be allowed to enter the city. He then proceeded with his companions to Padua, to get the testimony of a notary that the party was not stricken with the plague. Ignatius could not, on account of his weakness, keep pace with the others, and was left alone in an open field. Then Christ appeared to him, as He had appeared on former occasions. By this vision he was greatly strengthened and consoled. The next morning, filled with new courage, he came to the gate of the city, and although provided with no certificate, entered unquestioned by the guard. In the same way he left the city unquestioned. His companions were surprised at this, for they had to present a certificate, which he had taken no pains to procure. At Venice they begged their food, and slept in St Mark's Square. Ignatius refused to go to the house of the Ambassador, and although he made no effort to get money for his voyage to Jerusalem, he felt sure nevertheless that God would provide him with means.

One day he met a rich Spaniard, who asked him whither he was going, and having learned his intention, brought him to dine at his house. Here he remained for several days. From the time he left Manresa, Ignatius, while seated at table with others, had made it a practice never to speak except to give a brief answer to questions. However, he heard all that was said, and took occasion after dinner to give the conversation a spiritual turn. His host and all his family were so filled with admiration for him that they tried to induce him to remain with them, and introduced him to the Doge of Venice. The latter offered him accommodations on the government ship about to sail for Cyprus. Many pilgrims had assembled at Venice to go to Jerusalem, but the greater part hesitated through fear, as the Island of Rhodes had fallen into the hands of the Turks. Thirteen sailed in the pilgrims' ship, which was the first to weigh anchor. The government ship carried eight or nine. About the time of departure Ignatius was taken ill with a fever, which lasted several days. On the day of sailing he took the prescribed medicine, and asked the doctor if he could go. The doctor replied he could if he wished the vessel to be his tomb. Nevertheless he went on board, and after a fit of illness soon recovered.

The licentious conduct of those on board Ignatius severely censured. The Spaniards advised him not to do this, as the rest thought of abandoning him on an island. But the wind quickly conveyed them to Cyprus. From Cyprus they went to another port called Salinae, ten leagues distant. Here he went on board the ship of the pilgrims, with no other provision than his hope in Providence. During all that voyage, the Lord often appeared to him, and gave him great consolation. The visions seemed to take the form of something large, round, and golden. The travellers reached Joppa, and seated on asses, after the custom of that region, they journeyed to Jerusalem. A noble Spanish gentleman, named Didacus Minez, as the pilgrims came in sight of the city, recommended silence and recollection.

All followed his suggestion, and when they saw a monk approaching with a crucifix, dismounted. On beholding the city, Ignatius was deeply affected, and the rest affirmed that they experienced a sort of heavenly joy. He always felt this same devotion whenever he visited the holy places. He decided to remain in Jerusalem, in order to visit the holy places often. For this purpose he had taken with him letters of recommendation to the Father Guardian. On presenting them, he said that he intended to remain there to satisfy his own devotion, but said nothing of his purpose of helping others. The Father Guardian told him he did not see how this could be possible, as his house was not even capable of providing for his own Religious, and he intended to send some away from the Holy Land. Ignatius said he wished him merely to hear his confession, since he had come to make it. The Father Guardian said this could be done, but he should wait for the arrival of the Provincial, who was then at Bethlehem. Relying on this promise, Ignatius began to write letters to spiritual persons at Barcelona. He had written some on the day before he was to depart, when he was summoned in the name of the Father Guardian and the Provincial. Then the Provincial, addressing him kindly, said he had heard of his pious determination to remain in the holy places, and had given it serious thought. Many others had the same desire, some had died, others had been taken prisoners, and to his Order was left the work of ransoming captives, wherefore he should prepare himself to resume his journey with the pilgrims on the following day. To this Ignatius answered that his resolution was very fixed, and he did not think that anything would keep him from executing it. If the precept did not bind him under pain of sin, he would not allow any fear to keep him from carrying out his desire. The Provincial said he had authority from the Holy See to detain those he thought fit, and to even excommunicate those who would not obey when stopped by him, and he thought in this case it was better for him not to remain. When he wished to show the pontifical papers giving him power to excommunicate, Ignatius said there was no need, as he believed his word. If they had the authority, he would obey.

After this, returning to where he was before, he was seized with a great longing to visit Mount Olivet again before he departed, since the Divine Will would not suffer him to remain in those holy places. On that mountain is a rock from which Our Lord ascended to heaven, on which even now His footprints are visible. And this is what he wished to see again. Therefore, without telling anyone, and without a guide, although it was a dangerous thing to go without a Turkish guard, secretly withdrawing he went to Mount Olivet alone. As the guards would not allow him to enter, he gave them his knife. After great consolation in prayer he desired to go to Bethphage. When he reached that place, he thought that on Mount Olivet he had not noticed the position of the right foot of Our Lord and that of the left. He came a second time, and gave his scissors to the guards to allow him to enter. Afterward when at the monastery it was discovered he had gone without a guide, a great search was made for him. Coming down from Mount Olivet he met a girdled Christian, those who are bound to wear a girdle to distinguish them from the Mussulmans; this man, pretending to be very angry, threatened him with a large stick, and approaching, firmly grasped him by the arm. He allowed himself to be led, but the good man once he had hold of him did not let him go. In the meantime, as he was thus led along a captive, he was visited with great consolation, as he seemed to see Christ walking above him. And this continued until he reached the monastery.

CHAPTER V

HIS ARRIVAL IN APULIA, VENICE, FERRARA, AND GENOA—HE IS APPREHENDED AS A SPY—HE IS DESPISED AS A FOOL—HIS STUDIES AT BARCELONA AND ALCALA

On the following day the pilgrims took their departure, and arriving at Cyprus, were assigned to different vessels. In the harbour of that place were three or four ships bound for Venice. Of these one belonged to some Turks; another was too small; but the third, the property of a wealthy Venetian, was very large and strong.

Some of the band asked the captain of this last to take the pilgrim aboard; but, finding that no pay was to be offered, he refused, in spite of the fact that many begged him and were loud in their praises of the pilgrim. His reply was, that if the pilgrim were indeed a holy man, he might cross the sea as St James did.

The favour they asked was easily obtained of the captain of the smaller ship.

On a certain day they set sail with a favourable wind, but toward evening a storm arose, which tossed the vessels about in different directions. The large ship, whose captain had refused to take Ignatius, was driven by the tempest against the Island of Cyprus, and dashed to pieces. A like fate overtook the Turkish vessel. The small ship, however, though for a long time severely tried by wind and waves, finally reached the shores of Apulia in safety.

Although the winter had set in with intense cold and a heavy fall of snow, Ignatius had no garments save a pair of knee-breeches of a very rough texture, leaving the legs naked, a black waistcoat open and quite ragged about his shoulders, a light cloak made of coarse hair, and a pair of shoes. He arrived at Venice about the middle of January, having spent a good part of the preceding month and all of November aboard the ship which carried him from Cyprus.

At Venice, he met a friend who had been kind to him on his way to Jerusalem. From him he received alms and some cloth, which he wrapped about his body as a protection against the intense cold.

When Ignatius understood that God did not wish him to remain at Jerusalem, he began to consider what he should do. The plan he approved and adopted was to enter upon a course of study in order to be better fitted to save souls. For this purpose he determined to go to Barcelona, and setting out from Venice he travelled toward Genoa.

While praying at the principal church of Ferrara, he gave five or six coins to a beggar who asked an alms. To a second beggar he was equally generous. As soon as the beggars saw him so prodigal of his alms, they flocked around him, until he had spent all the money that he had; so when others approached to ask for assistance, he excused himself on the plea that he had nothing left.

While proceeding from Ferrara to Genoa, he met some Spanish soldiers, who treated him kindly, and who were not a little surprised at his choosing such a route, since by so doing he was compelled to pass through the very midst of the armies of France and Spain. They entreated him therefore to take a safer road, which they would point out to him, and to withdraw from the highway.

Not following their counsel, however, he kept straight on until he came to a town fortified by strong walls. Seized as a spy, the guards cast him into a small house not far from the gate, and, as is customary in such suspicious times, closely questioned him. On all points, however, he professed the greatest ignorance. Finally they searched his clothes and shoes to see if he bore any messages, and finding nothing, they led him into the presence of the captain. They deprived him of his cloak, leaving him only his waistcoat and knee-breeches.

As he was compelled to go about in this condition, he recalled to mind the thought of Christ led about as a captive. Although he was forced to walk through the three principal streets of the town, he did so, not with sadness, but feeling great joy and consolation.

In addressing others he was in the habit of saying '*you*,' employing no other word either of reverence or dignity, believing that such was the simplicity as well of the Apostles as of Christ Himself.

While being conducted through the different streets, it occurred to him that it would be well to depart somewhat from his ordinary custom, and to show greater respect to the commander of the place. Such a thought was by no means the outcome of the fear of any punishment which they might inflict. He felt, however, that this was a temptation; he said, 'In that case I'll neither address him as a person of dignity, nor bend the knee as a mark of respect, nor even remove my hat in his presence.'

Having reached the residence of the commander, he was made to wait some time in the courtyard before being summoned into his presence. Then, without manifesting the slightest degree of civility, he so paused after each word he spoke as to be taken for a fool by the commander, who said to his captors, 'This man is an idiot; restore what belongs to him and send him away.'

A certain Spaniard met Ignatius coming from the house of the commander, led him home, just as he was, and gave him food and whatever was necessary for that night.

The next morning he resumed his journey until toward evening, when, espied by the soldiers of a fort, he was seized and brought to the commander of the French forces. The latter, among other things, asked where he came from. When Ignatius answered, 'Guipuscoa,' the officer said, 'I also come from near that place'; and immediately he ordered Ignatius to be conducted within to supper and to be treated with great kindness.

At Genoa, he was recognised by a Cantabrian, who had spoken with him elsewhere, when in the army of his Catholic Majesty. Through his influence, he was taken on a ship bound for Barcelona. He came very near being taken captive by Andrea Dorea, who was at that time in the service of the French, and gave chase to the vessel.

At Barcelona, he was enabled to study through the assistance of a noble and very pious lady, Isabel Roser, and a teacher, named Ardebal. Both highly approved his plan, Ardebal promising to give him instruction free, while Isabel generously offered to provide him with everything necessary.

At Manresa, there was a very holy monk, of the Order of St Bernard, with whom Ignatius wished to remain, as well for his own personal guidance as to prepare himself to direct others. He accordingly accepted the offer of his two generous friends on condition that what he sought could not be obtained at Manresa. Finding, however, that the monk had died, he returned to Barcelona and applied himself to study. In this, however, he was destined to meet with some difficulties. In his studies, the principles of grammar caused new spiritual thoughts and tastes to arise so abundantly, as to render him incapable of committing anything to memory, and though he strove hard, he could not dispel these thoughts.

Noticing, however, that while praying at Mass he did not experience similar thoughts, he considered this a temptation. Accordingly, after praying for some time, he asked his teacher to come to the Church of Blessed Mary of the

Sea, not far from the professor's house, and there to listen to what he would tell him. Ignatius faithfully made known the whole state of his mind, and why he had as yet learned so little. 'But,' he said, 'I promise not to be wanting in attention in school during these two years, provided that at Barcelona I may be able to find bread and water.'

Such an acknowledgment was of the greatest efficacy, and he never after experienced that temptation. The pains of the stomach, which afflicted him at Manresa, ceased, and, in fact, they did not trouble him from the time he set out for Jerusalem.

While studying at Barcelona, he wished to practise his former penances. Accordingly, making a hole in the soles of his shoes, he tore them, little by little, until nothing but the upper portion was left.

His two years of study being completed, in which, they say, he greatly advanced, he was advised by his master to go to Alcala to study philosophy, as he was deemed ready for it.

Before setting out, however, he wished to be examined by a certain theologian. As he also gave him the same advice, Ignatius, unaccompanied, started for Alcala. Here he began to beg and live upon alms. After ten or twelve days, this kind of life drew upon him the contempt of a priest and of some others. They began to insult him as one who preferred to live on alms, although quite able to support himself.

The superior of a new hospital, seeing him thus rudely treated, took him home, placed him in a room, and liberally provided for his needs.

The time of his arrival at Barcelona was about Lent of the year 1524; and as he remained there upwards of two years, we do not find him at Alcala until the year 1526. At the latter place he spent his time in studying the works of Scotus, Albertus, Alcuin, and the Master of the Sentences. He was diligent also in giving the Spiritual Exercises and explaining the Christian doctrine, by which he gave great glory to God, as very many were thereby led to a knowledge and taste of spiritual things. Many, however, fell victims to various temptations, an example of which is to be seen in one who was unable to scourge himself, because, as he fancied, his hand was held by some invisible agent. Because of such affairs, and especially by reason of the great crowd of men coming to him when he explained the Christian doctrine, various rumours began to spread among the people.

When he first came to Alcala a friendship sprang up between him and one Didacus Guya, who lived with his brother, a painter. Through that friendship, Ignatius was abundantly supplied with all that was necessary; hence he would bestow upon the poor the alms that he himself obtained, and besides three other pilgrims stayed with him.

One day Ignatius went to Didacus to ask for alms in order to assist some poor people. He replied that he had no money. Opening, however, a chest which belonged to him, he took from it trappings of various colours, candlesticks, and other objects, which he gave to Ignatius, who distributed them to the poor.

Many rumours, as was stated above, became widespread in Alcala, and reached the ears even of the Inquisitors who were at Toledo, and who, as their host testified, styled Ignatius and his associates, Legati or Illuminati, and threatened him with capital punishment.

The Inquisitors who had come to Alcala to investigate their actions left the entire affair in the hands of the Vicar Figueroa, who was then negotiating with the Emperor, and returned to Toledo without having even once summoned them. Figueroa granted them the right to continue the work in which they were engaged, and the Inquisitors, after mature deliberation, discovered error neither in their doctrines nor in their manner of life.

They did not, however, favour their custom of dressing alike, as they were not Religious. Ignatius replied that the wish of the Vicar would be obeyed, but he added: 'I do not see the fruit of these examinations, since but a few days ago a certain priest refused holy communion to one, on the plea that he had communicated but eight days before; and to me, indeed, he gave it very reluctantly. We would like to know whether or not we have been guilty of any heresy?' 'None,' replied Figueroa, 'else you would have been led to the stake.' 'And they would likewise have led you to the stake,' responded Ignatius, 'had you been convicted of heresy.'

The dress was changed according to the wish of Figueroa, who also desired that the pilgrim should not go around barefooted for at least fifteen or twenty days. This command was also obeyed.

Four months after, Figueroa, a second time, brought the Inquisition to bear upon them, influenced, as I think, by the fact that a certain married woman of rank, who chanced to be singularly devoted to the pilgrim, went in disguise at daybreak to visit Ignatius at the hospital where he was staying. But even on this occasion Ignatius was not summoned to appear before the Inquisition; nor was any sentence pronounced against him.

CHAPTER VI

THE PRISONS AT ALCALA AND SALAMANCA

After the space of four months, Ignatius, who did not remain at the hospital, was taken from his lodging by a public officer, who cast him into prison, with the command not to depart until otherwise ordered.

This took place during the summer months, and as the discipline of the prison was not very strict, an opportunity of visiting him was afforded many persons, to whom he explained the principles of Christian faith and the Exercises, as was his wont when enjoying perfect freedom.

Many persons of rank were anxious to help him, but he did not wish to avail himself of their offers. One person especially, Lady Teresa de Cardena, sent frequently, offering to deliver him from prison. He replied in these words, "He, for whose love I am imprisoned, will free me when it may be His good pleasure."

He passed seventeen days in prison,—yet was totally ignorant of the cause,—when Figueroa came to question him. Among other things, he asked whether he commanded the observance of the Sabbath.

Among those who had frequently come to see Ignatius were two persons, a mother and daughter, the latter of whom was young and beautiful. These, especially the daughter, had made great progress in the spiritual life, and although ladies of rank, had determined to make a pilgrimage alone and on foot, and beg their way to the shrine of Veronica, in the city of Jaen.

This occasioned so great a sensation throughout the city of Alcala that Dr. Giruellus, who was the guardian of the two women, thinking that Ignatius was the cause of their action, ordered him to be cast into prison.

As the Vicar was willing to be fully informed, Ignatius said: 'These women made known to me their desire of going about from place to place to assist the poor they found in the different hospitals. I, however, disapproved of their design, on account of the daughter, who was quite young and beautiful, representing to them at the same time that if they felt strongly urged to assist the poor, Alcala presented a broad enough field for their labours, and they could satisfy their devotion by accompanying the Blessed Sacrament as it was being carried to the sick.' When Ignatius had finished his account, Figueroa and the notary departed, after writing down what had taken place.

Calisto, a companion of Ignatius, and who on recovering from a severe illness had heard of the imprisonment of Ignatius, hastened from Segovia, where he was staying, and came to Alcala, that he, too, might be cast into prison.

Ignatius advised him to go to the Vicar, who received him kindly, and promised to send him to prison. It was necessary, he said, for him to be detained until the return of the women. It could then be seen whether or not their account agreed with what he and Ignatius had stated.

As the confinement was undermining Calisto's health, Ignatius, through the intervention of a professor who was a friend of his, obtained his liberation.

When Ignatius had been in prison forty-two days, the women returned. He was once more visited by the notary, who made known to him the condition on which he was to regain his freedom. It was this: He and his companions should wear the same style of clothing as the other students, and refrain from preaching the truths of faith until they had finished four more years of study. Ignatius, indeed, had made more progress in his studies than the rest, yet he confessed that he had not been solidly grounded. And this he was always wont to say whenever he was questioned.

When Ignatius heard the judgment passed upon himself and his companions, he was at a loss what to do, for he saw very little chance of advancing the salvation of souls, hindered as he was for no other reason than that of not having completed a full course of study.

He finally resolved to trust the entire affair to the good sense and judgment of Fonseca, Archbishop of Toledo, whom, after leaving Alcala, he found at Valladolid.

To the Archbishop, then, he made known everything with the utmost fidelity, and said that, although it was not a matter pertaining either to his court or judgment, he determined to act as the Archbishop should advise.

The Archbishop received him cordially, approving his intention of going to Salamanca, and assuring him that he would find friends there. Supplying him with everything necessary for his journey, he dismissed him.

When sentence had been pronounced against them at Alcala, Ignatius promised obedience, but at the same time observed that they were too poor to provide themselves with new clothing. Hearing this, the Vicar himself supplied what they needed, and they set out for Alcala.

Four of his companions had already taken up their abode at Salamanca. When he reached the city Ignatius went to church to pray, and was recognised by a pious lady, who, asking his name, conducted him to his companions. About ten or twelve days after their arrival at Salamanca, a Dominican monk, to whom Ignatius had made his confession, pressed him to visit the convent, as some of the Religious wished to see him.

Ignatius accepting the invitation 'in the name of the Lord,' his confessor thought it well for him to come to dine the Sunday following, at the same time adding that many questions would be put to him. On Sunday, therefore, as was appointed, the pilgrim came in company with Calisto.

When dinner was over, the Superior, together with the confessor and others, conducted Ignatius to a chapel, and after expressing his pleasure at the good account received of him and his apostolic zeal, manifested a desire of hearing a more full and exact account of his teaching.

He was first questioned in reference to his studies. Ignatius answered that he had spent more time in studying than his companions, yet he confessed that his knowledge was not very extensive, as he had never laid a solid foundation.

'Why, then, do you preach?' broke in the monk. 'We do not preach,' replied Ignatius; 'we are wont to talk familiarly about divine things with some, in much the same as after dinner we converse with our host.'

'About what divine things?' continued the monk; 'this is the very point upon which we wish information.'

'About different virtues and vices,' rejoined Ignatius, 'endeavouring to inculcate a love of virtue and a detestation of vice.'

'How comes it,' said the monk, 'that you who are not learned should presume to converse upon virtue and vice? No one is wont to engage in such a task unless he has acquired knowledge or has been taught by the Holy Ghost. You confess ignorance of letters; it follows then that He has been your director. We wish to learn, therefore, what He has been pleased to make known to you.'

Ignatius at first made no reply, as he felt such reasoning was without value. Soon, however, breaking the silence, he remarked that there seemed no reason why he should say more upon the subject. As the monk still pressed him, giving as a reason the fact that many were once more thrusting forward the erroneous doctrine of Erasmus and others, Ignatius answered, 'I will add no more to what has already been said, unless questioned by those who have a right to expect an account from me.'

Previous to the present proceedings the monk wished to know why Calisto was so strangely clothed, for, although of tall stature, he went about almost barelegged, holding a staff in his hand, and wearing a cloak much too short, and a hat of enormous size. The whole costume formed a rather ludicrous picture.

Ignatius replied that although at Alcala they were ordered to dress as the other students, Calisto had charitably given his clothes to a poor priest.

The monk showed himself displeased at this, remarking, 'Charity begins at home.'

But to return to our former narrative. When the monk saw Ignatius fixed in his resolution, 'You shall remain here,' he said, 'and we shall easily find a way of compelling you to make everything known.' Immediately all the monks withdrew, the subprior signifying his wish that Ignatius should remain in the chapel. The matter was then laid before the judges. Both Ignatius and Calisto remained three days in the monastery, taking their meals with the community, before any decision of the judges was made known to them. During this time the Religious frequently visited their cells, and Ignatius never failed to speak with them in his accustomed manner. This caused the monks to be divided in their opinion of him, and many, indeed, showed themselves very kindly disposed.

On the third day a notary came to conduct them to prison. They were not put with the common criminals, but their place of confinement was nevertheless very repulsive. In the centre of the cell there was a pillar to which was attached a chain but a few feet in length, and so riveted to the prisoners that when either moved the other was obliged to follow him. They passed that night without any sleep. On the following day, however, the report spread that they were prisoners. The people then hastened to supply them with all they needed.

Ignatius, as may readily be supposed, lost no opportunity of speaking upon spiritual things with those who came to see them.

They were each separately examined by a friar, to whom Ignatius delivered all his writings. Among these were his Spiritual Exercises, that it might be seen whether or not they contained any false doctrine. When asked about his other companions, he told who and where they were. They were arrested also, and confined in separate apartments from that in which Ignatius was placed.

Although help was offered on this occasion, he declined to accept it.

After a few days he was called into the presence of the judges and professors, who made him answer many questions, not only on his Spiritual Exercises, but even on articles of faith, as, for example, the Trinity and the Blessed Sacrament, requiring him to explain these mysteries.

So clear and exact was his explanation that his examiners could not find the least flaw in his doctrine. He was equally correct in the answer to the friar who proposed a difficulty in Canon Law.

In every case he said that he did not know the decision of the professors.

When ordered to speak on the first commandment, he gave so full and exhaustive an explanation as to leave to his hearers no further chance of questioning him.

Although he had not completed his studies, he frequently showed the difference between a mortal and a venial sin of thought. While speaking about his Exercises, he was closely questioned. To their questions, however, he replied, 'What I say is either false or true; if false, condemn it.' The doctrine remained uncondemned.

Francis de Mendoza, afterward Cardinal of Valencia, was one of those who came to the prison to visit Ignatius. One day, while accompanied with the friar, he asked him whether the prison and chains were not insupportable. 'I shall give,' said Ignatius, 'the reply made today to a woman who bewailed my lot. For the love of Jesus Christ, I gladly would wear all the handcuffs and chains that could be found in Salamanca. And if you consider this an evil, you show that as yet you are not desirous of suffering imprisonment for the love of Our Lord.'

About this time it happened that all the inmates of the prison managed to escape, leaving only Ignatius and his companions. When this became known it caused a reaction in their favour, and they were placed for the time in a large building adjoining the prison.

On the twenty-second day of their imprisonment they were summoned to hear their sentence.

Although they were declared to be free from reproach both in their lives and their doctrines, and were allowed to continue their work of teaching the Christian doctrine and of speaking on spiritual subjects, yet they were forbidden to draw any distinction between mortal and venial sin, until they should have spent four more years in study.

Although Ignatius was unwilling to accept the sentence, because, though condemned in no respect, he was nevertheless prevented from assisting his neighbour, he declared that he would submit as long as he remained in Salamanca.

Recommending the affair to God, Ignatius began to deliberate on his future plan of action. He considered it a waste of time to remain at Salamanca, as the restriction laid upon him prevented him from assisting those for whose salvation he wished to labour.

He resolved, accordingly, to set out for Paris for the purpose of there continuing his studies.

While studying at Barcelona, Ignatius was in doubt whether, after completing his studies, he should enter some Religious Order, or go from place to place, according to his custom.

He decided to enter upon the religious life. His next step was to find some Order where the primitive fervour had not relaxed, as he felt that there he would be more sure of satisfying his desire of suffering and assisting others spiritually by bearing, for the love of God, any injury or insult to which he might be subjected.

Even while at Salamanca these desires were ever present to him. To this end he directed all his studies, endeavouring at the same time to persuade others to adopt a like course, and to strengthen in their good resolutions those who had already embraced it.

When he had resolved to go to Paris, he communicated his design to his companions, telling them to remain where they were, until he could find a means of helping them in their studies.

Many persons of rank endeavoured to dissuade him from departing, but all to no purpose.

Placing the few books he possessed upon a little ass, he took leave of his companions about fifteen or twenty days after they came out of prison.

Those who met him at Barcelona sought to deter him from going to France, as at that time the war between the two countries was raging with great fierceness. Notwithstanding the many acts of cruelty inflicted by the French upon the Spaniards, many of whom had been impaled, he persevered in his intention.

CHAPTER VII

HIS STUDIES IN PARIS, AND OTHER INCIDENTS OF HIS LIFE

He left for Paris on foot and alone, and, according to his own reckoning, arrived there toward the beginning of February, 1528. While in prison, the Prince of Spain was born, and from this event we can determine the date of what preceded and followed. At Paris he lived with some Spaniards, and attended the lectures given at the College of Montaigu. As he had been advanced too rapidly to the higher studies, he returned to those of a lower grade, because he felt that in great part he lacked the proper groundwork. He therefore studied in a class with children. When he first came to Paris, he received from a merchant twenty-five gold crowns on an order sent from Barcelona. These he put for safekeeping in the hands of one of the Spaniards with whom he lived. This latter very soon appropriated them for his own use, and when called upon, could not restore them. The result was that when Lent was over Ignatius found himself unprovided for, partly on account of the loss mentioned, and partly on account of other expenses.

In consequence, he was forced to seek his livelihood by begging, and to leave the house where he lived.

Afterward he was received into the Hospital of St James, near the Church of the Holy Innocents. This residence proved no slight hindrance to his studies. The hospital was at a great distance from the college, and while he could not gain admission at night unless he returned before the sound of the Angelus, in the morning he was not allowed to depart before daylight. He could not, in consequence, be present at, nor give his time to, the lectures with profit. He found another hindrance, also, in loss of the time needed in getting alms wherewith to purchase food.

As he had not experienced interior spiritual suffering for almost five years, he mortified himself by austere fasts and penances. After he had spent some time in this way, living in the hospital and begging his food, he noticed that his progress in letters was not rapid. He then considered what course to follow. He had observed that many who lived as servants of the lecturers in the colleges had abundant time for study. He resolved to seek someone whom he might serve in the same way. He weighed the matter well, and not without consolation thought of it as follows: 'I shall imagine that my master is Christ, and I shall call one of the students Peter, another John, and to the rest I shall give the names of the remaining Apostles. Then, when my master gives me a command, I shall think, that Christ commands me. When any one else gives orders, I shall think that the order comes from St Peter or some other Apostle.' He was very diligent in seeking a master, and spoke of the matter to a bachelor and to a Carthusian monk, who knew many masters, and to others, but he was never able to find one.

Deprived of every resource, he was told by a Spanish monk that it would be a wise step for him to go every year to Flanders, and there in two months he could procure enough for the whole year. He approved of the plan, after recommending the matter to God. On adopting this plan, he brought back yearly from Flanders whatever he needed for his maintenance. Once even he passed over into England, and from there brought greater alms than he had gathered in the previous years.

When he first returned from Flanders he began to devote himself earnestly to spiritual work. About the same time he gave the Exercises to three persons,—to Peralta, to Castro, a friend who dwelt at Sorbonne, and to a Cantabrian who lived in the College of St Barbara, by name Amator. A great change was made in the lives of these men. At once they gave to the poor whatever they had, even their books, while they themselves began to live on the alms they begged, and to dwell in the Hospital of St James, where Ignatius had previously dwelt, and which he left as stated above. This incident aroused a great outcry in the University of Paris, because the two first were very famous men. The other Spaniards at once undertook to oppose them, but unable to persuade them by any argument to return to the university, a great crowd went armed to the hospital and led, or rather dragged, them away.

On coming to the university they agreed with their captors to complete their course of studies, and afterward to follow out their determination. Castro went afterward to Spain, and after preaching for a while at Burgos, joined the Order of the Carthusians at Valencia. Peralta undertook a journey to Jerusalem on foot and after the fashion of a pilgrim. In this garb he was seized in Italy by a military leader, his relative, who found a pretext for bringing him before the Sovereign Pontiff, from whom he obtained a command for Peralta to return to Spain. All these events did not occur then, but years afterward. Exaggerated reports arose against Ignatius at Paris, especially among the Spaniards. De Govea was wont to say that Amator, who remained in his college, had been brought by Ignatius to the verge of insanity. He therefore made up his mind that as soon as Ignatius came to the College of St Barbara, he would give him a public whipping as a seducer of the pupils.

Now the Spaniard who had spent the money of Ignatius and had not paid him, had set out to journey to Spain and fallen sick. As soon as Ignatius learned of this, he was seized with a longing to visit and help him, hoping by this to lead him to abandon the world and give himself wholly to God. And indeed to accomplish this he wished to make the journey barefooted, without food or drink. While praying for this purpose, he felt himself seized with great fear until, entering the Church of St Dominic, he resolved to make the journey in this manner. The fear that it might be tempting God then left him; on the morning of the following day, upon arising, so great a fear seized him that it seemed to him that he could not even put on his clothes. In this interior strife he left the house and went out of the city, and the fear did not leave him till he was nine miles from Paris. At this distance there is a village which the inhabitants call Argenteuil, where the Holy Coat of Our Lord is said to be preserved. As he left this place in great trouble of spirit, a feeling of great consolation and strength filled his soul with such joy that he began to shout aloud and to talk with God as he walked through the fields. That night, having completed forty-five miles, he went to rest with a beggar in a hospital. On the next day toward nightfall he lodged in a straw-thatched cabin. On the third day he arrived on foot. According to his resolve, he took neither food nor drink. Upon his arrival he consoled the sick man, helped him on board a vessel which was about to sail for Spain, and gave him letters to his companions, Calisto, Caceres, and Artiaga, who were in Salamanca. Here we may dwell for a moment on the fate of these companions. While Ignatius was at Paris he often sent them letters, telling them of the little hope left of calling them to Paris for their studies. Still he urged by letter Donna Leonora de Mascarenas to use her influence with the King of Portugal for Calisto, that he might receive one of the burses which the King had established. A certain yearly aid is called a burse. Donna Leonora gave Calisto a mule and money to take him to the court of the King of Portugal. He set out, but never reached that place. He came back afterward to Spain and went to India. He returned rich, to the great surprise of all at Salamanca, who had known him in former days. Caceres, after returning to Segovia, his native city, began to grow unmindful of his former purpose and life. Artiaga was first made a magistrate. Afterward, when the Society was established at Rome, a bishopric was given to him. He wrote to Ignatius, 'I wish this bishopric to be given to one of the Society.' But as soon as the answer came that this was not to be done, he went to India, was made bishop, and died there a strange death. While sick it chanced that two phials of liquid were placed in water to cool, one containing a medicine ordered for him by the doctor, the other a diluted poison called Sollimanus. His attendant gave him by mistake the poisoned draught, which he drank, and thus ended his life.

Returning to Paris Ignatius heard many rumours connecting his name with that of Caceres and Peralta, and learned that he had been summoned before the judge. As he did not wish to remain in doubt, he went of his own accord to the Inquisitor, a Dominican friar. 'I heard that I had been sought for, and I now present myself.' During the conversation he asked the Inquisitor to terminate the matter speedily. He had determined to begin his course in arts on the approaching feast of St Remigius, and therefore wished all other business completed in order to apply himself to his studies with greater profit. The Inquisitor on his part told him that it was true that certain charges had been made against him, but he allowed him to depart, and did not summon him again.

Toward the first of October, the feast of St Remigius, he began his course under the preceptor Master John Pegna, with the intention of fostering the vocations of those who wished to serve God. He intended to add others in order the more freely to give his mind to his studies. He followed the lectures in philosophy, and experienced the same temptations with which he had been assailed when studying grammar at Barcelona. During the lectures he was troubled by so many spiritual thoughts that he could not listen attentively. Accordingly, as he saw he was making but little progress in his studies, he spoke to his preceptor and promised to attend the lectures, as long as he could find bread and water enough to keep him alive. After making this promise, all these untimely devotions ceased to disturb him, and he quietly pursued his studies. He was at this period a friend of Peter Faber and Francis Xavier, whom he afterward led to the service of God by giving them the Exercises. During the last years he was not persecuted as at first. Speaking of this to him one day, Doctor Fragus remarked that he was surprised that no one molested him. Ignatius replied: 'This is owing to the fact that I do not speak on religious topics. But when the course is completed, we shall act as formerly.'

During the course of this conversation a monk approached Doctor Fragus and begged his aid in visiting a house, in which there were many corpses of those whom he thought died of the plague. At that time the plague was beginning to spread in Paris. Doctor Fragus and Ignatius wished to visit the house, and procured the aid of a woman who was very skilful in detecting the disease. After she had entered the house she answered that the plague was certainly there. Ignatius, also, entered and consoled and revived a sick man he found lying there. When he had touched the wounds with his hand, Ignatius departed alone. His hand began to cause him great pain, and it seemed as if he had caught the disease. The fear that came upon him was so great that he was unable to vanquish and drive it away, until with a great effort he placed his fingers in his mouth, and for a long time kept them there, saying, 'If you have the plague in your hand, you will also have it in your mouth.' As soon as this was done, the illusion left him and the pain he had felt in his hand ceased.

He was not allowed to enter the College of St Barbara where he was then living, for all fled from him when they learned that he had entered a house infected with the plague. He was obliged to remain several days outside of the college.

At Paris it is customary for those who follow the philosophical studies to receive in their third year the Petra, as it is called, in order to obtain the bachelor's degree. Now those who are very poor are unable to comply with this custom, as it costs a gold crown. While Ignatius was in great hesitation, he submitted the matter to the judgment of his preceptor. The latter advised him to receive it. He did so, but not without a complaint on the part of some, especially of a certain Spaniard who had taken note of the fact.

While in Paris he suffered great pains of the stomach for several days. On the twenty-fifth day, for the space of an hour, a very severe pain seized him, bringing with it a fever. One day the pains lasted for sixteen or seventeen hours. At that time he had already concluded his course, had spent some years in the study of theology, and had collected his companions.

As the disease grew worse day by day, and the many remedies employed brought no relief, the doctors said that the only one left for him was to revisit his native land, as nothing but his native air could cure him. His companions gave him the same advice. By this time all had determined on their future conduct, namely, to go first to Venice, and then to Jerusalem, where they would pass their whole life in helping souls. If, however, they should not be allowed to remain in Jerusalem, they were to return to Rome and offer themselves to the Sovereign Pontiff, Christ's Vicar, that he might use their aid as he thought would be for God's glory and the salvation of souls. They also agreed to wait one year at Venice for ships to carry them to the Holy Land; but if during the year no ship were at hand, they should be absolved from the vow, and go to the Sovereign Pontiff. Finally Ignatius yielded to the advice of his companions, in order to attend to their business in Spain. It was agreed among them, that after the recovery of his health he should settle their affairs and they should go to Venice, and there await him.

He left Paris in the year 1535, but according to the agreement his companions were to leave two years afterward on the feast of the conversion of St Paul. However, owing to the wars, they were obliged to anticipate that time, and to set out from Paris in the month of November in the year 1536. On the very eve of his departure, as Ignatius had heard that an accusation had been made against him before the Inquisitor, while no summons had as yet been served, he went to that official and stated what he had heard. At the same time he told him that he had several companions, and that he himself was about to travel to Spain, and requested that sentence should be passed upon him. The Inquisitor admitted that the accusation had been made, but that he did not think it worthy of consideration. He said that he wished merely to see the writings of Ignatius, meaning the Exercises. Having seen these he approved of them very highly, and begged Ignatius to give him a copy. Ignatius complied with his request, but insisted that his trial be brought to an end, and that judgment be passed. As his request met with a refusal, he brought a notary and witnesses to the Inquisitor's house, and received their testimony in writing concerning his innocence of the charges.

CHAPTER VIII

HIS ARRIVAL IN HIS NATIVE LAND AND THE VIRTUES PRAC-
TISED THERE—HIS JOURNEY INTO SPAIN AND ITALY—THE
FAMOUS APPARITION AND HIS LIFE IN THE SAME PLACE

After the event related in the last chapter, Ignatius mounted the little horse which his companions had purchased for him, and began his journey toward his native land. Even on the way he found his health improving. As soon as he arrived in the province of Guipuscoa, his native country, abandoning the common highway he followed a road through the mountains because it was less frequented. He had advanced a short distance by this path when he saw two armed men approaching. The place was famous as the haunt of murderers. The men passed him a little and then turning, hurried after him. He was not a little frightened, but still, addressing them, he learned that they were his brother's servants sent to meet him. For he had reason to believe that a warning of his coming was sent to his brother from Bayonne in France, where he had been recognised by several persons. Still Ignatius kept on in the direction he had taken, and shortly before he arrived in the town he met some priests coming to meet him. They wished to bring him to his brother's home; but their efforts were unavailing. He went to a public hospital, and afterward, at a suitable time, begged for alms through the town.

Many came to see him in the hospital. He spoke to them, and through God's grace gathered no little fruit. Upon his arrival, he resolved to teach the Christian doctrine to children every day. His brother objected to this, and assured him that no one would come. In answer Ignatius said, 'One is enough for me.' However, as soon as he began to teach, many came regularly, his brother among the number. In addition to this, on Sundays and feast days, he also preached to the people with great fruit, and thousands came many miles to hear him. He laboured also for the removal of many abuses, and through God's grace good results were obtained in many cases. To give an example: By his representations to the governor he obtained an order forbidding gambling and other disorders, under great penalties. He took means that the poor should be provided for publicly and regularly, and that thrice a day, morning, noon, and evening, according to the Roman custom, a signal should be given by ringing a bell for the recital of the Angelus by the people.

Although at first he enjoyed good health, he afterward fell seriously ill. For this reason, after his recovery, he determined to depart in order to accomplish the business which he had undertaken for his companions. He resolved to set out on foot and without money. His brother was grieved at this, and looked on it as a disgrace to himself. Ignatius concluded to yield this point, and at last, toward evening, he consented to be carried to the boundary of the province in company with his brother and relatives.

But as soon as he had left the province, he dismounted and without receiving any sustenance for the journey he set out for Pamplona and thence to Almazonus, the birthplace of Father Laynez. Then he travelled on to Siguensa and to Toledo, and afterward from Toledo to Valencia. In all these cities, the birthplaces of his companions, he would receive nothing from their parents and relations, although they offered him a great many things, and begged him to accept them. At Valencia he had a conversation with Castro. When ready to embark at Valencia to sail to Genoa, several of his well-wishers dissuaded him, because, as they asserted, the Barbary pirates were on the sea with many large ships. However, though they said a great deal to inspire fear, still he did not hesitate. Having gone aboard a vessel, a great storm arose during the voyage. This was mentioned before, where Ignatius describes the three occasions on which he was in danger of death. On this journey he suffered a great deal, as I shall now relate. One day after landing he wandered from his path and followed a road which ran along the bank of a river. The road was high, while far below was the river deep and sluggish. The farther he advanced, the narrower grew the road. At last he came to a spot where he could neither go forward nor backward. He then began to advance on hands and feet and continued thus for a long time, full of fear. For as often as he moved it seemed to him that he would fall into the river. This was the greatest of all the bodily labours that he ever experienced. At last he escaped, but just as he was entering Bologna he fell from a little bridge and was so wet and dirty from the mud and water as to afford much laughter to a great crowd who observed the accident. From his entrance into Bologna until his departure he begged for alms, and though he went through the whole city, he did not receive so much as a farthing. As he was ill, he rested for a while at Bologna. Thence he directed his steps toward Venice, travelling always in the same way. At Venice he spent his time in giving the Exercises and in other spiritual works. Those to whom he gave the Exercises were Peter Contarenus, Gaspar a Doctis, Rozes a Spaniard, and another Spaniard named Hozes, who, like the pilgrim, was a great friend of the bishop. Hozes at first would not make the Exercises, although he felt drawn to do so. At last he resolved to undertake the work, and on the third or fourth day he opened his mind to Ignatius. He said that he had feared that by the Exercises his mind might be imbued with false doctrines. Indeed, he had been persuaded by a man to be on his guard, and for this reason he had brought along with him a book to use in case he were imposed on. He made great progress in the Exercises, and finally embraced that manner of life which Ignatius had established. He was the first of the companions of the Saint to die.

At Venice another persecution was stirred up against Ignatius. Some asserted that he had been burned in effigy both in Spain and in Paris. The matter went so far that he was brought to trial, but obtained a favourable sentence. At the beginning of the year 1538 the nine companions came to Venice and were scattered about the city in various hospitals to minister to the sick. After two or three months all journeyed to Rome to receive the Pope's blessing before going to Jerusalem. Ignatius, however, did not go to Rome on account of Doctor Ortiz and the Theatine Cardinal recently raised to that dignity. The companions on their return brought the value of two or three hundred gold crowns which had been given to them as alms for their projected journey to Jerusalem. They would accept it only in the form of bills, and when they were unable to make the voyage to Jerusalem they returned it to those who had made the gift. They returned to Venice in the same manner that they had set out for Rome. They travelled on foot and begging, divided into three parties, as they were of different nationalities. Those who were not priests were ordained at Venice, having received faculties from the Nuncio, who was then in that city and who was afterward called Cardinal Verallus. They were promoted to the priesthood *sub titulo paupertatis*, having made vows of poverty and chastity. That year no ships left for the East, on account of the breach of the treaty between the Venetians and Turks. When, therefore, they saw their hopes deferred, they dispersed into various parts of the Venetian territory, with the understanding that they should wait one year, as they had previously resolved; when that time had elapsed, they were to return to Rome if it was not possible to make the voyage. Vicenza fell to the lot of Ignatius. His companions were Faber and Laynez. Outside of the city they found a house that had neither door nor windows. Here they lived, sleeping on a little straw which they had brought with them. Two of the three entered the city twice daily, in the morning and evening, to ask for alms. They returned with so little that it hardly sufficed for their nourishment. Their usual food was bread, when they could get it. The one who chanced to remain at home did the baking. In this way they spent forty days, intent upon nothing but prayer.

After the forty days were over, Master John Codurus arrived, and the four determined to begin preaching. On the same day and at the same hour, in different squares, all began to preach, having first uttered a great cry, and having waved their hats with their hands to call the people. These sermons caused great talk in the city, and led many citizens to a devout life. Now the needed nourishment was supplied to them more abundantly. While the pilgrim was at Vicenza, he had many spiritual visions. Consolations were sent to him in great number. This was especially so at Venice, while he was preparing for the priesthood and for celebrating Mass. On all his journeys, he received great supernatural visitations, like those which he had been wont to receive at Manresa.

While still at Venice he learned that one of his companions was sick unto death at Bassanum. He was himself ill with fever, still he undertook the journey, and walked so rapidly that Faber, his companion, was unable to keep up with him. On the way he received an assurance from God that his companion would not die of this illness. As soon as they arrived at Bassanum, the sick man was very much consoled, and not long after grew better. After this, all returned to Vicenza, and there the ten tarried for a while, some going about the neighbouring towns to beg for alms.

In the year that passed, as no means could be had of journeying to Jerusalem, they set out on their way to Rome, divided into three or four parties. On the journey Ignatius experienced singular visitations from God. After his reception of the priesthood, he had resolved to put off the offering of his first Mass for one year, in order to prepare himself better, and to ask the Most Blessed Virgin to place him near her Son. One day, when he was a few miles from Rome, he entered a church to pray, and there felt his soul so moved and changed, and saw so clearly that God the Father placed him with Christ His Son, that he did not dare to doubt it. When Ignatius was told that several other details were related by Laynez, he replied: 'Whatever Laynez said about the matter is true. For my part, I do not remember the particulars; but,' he added, 'I know for certain that when I related what happened I told nothing but the truth.' These were his words about the vision. He referred me to Laynez to verify what he narrated.

Once Ignatius left Rome for Monte Cassino, to give the Exercises to Doctor Ortiz, and spent forty days there. One day, at a certain hour, in a vision, he saw Hozes entering heaven. In this vision he shed abundant tears of consolation. He saw this so clearly that if he were to say the contrary, it would seem to him as if he were telling a lie. He brought with him from Monte Cassino Francis Strada. After his return to Rome, he laboured for the help of souls, and gave the Exercises to two different persons, one of whom dwelt near the Sixtine Bridge, the other near the Church of St Mary Major. Soon the people began to persecute Ignatius and his companions. Michael was the first of all to be troublesome and to speak wickedly of Ignatius, and had him summoned before the governor for trial. Ignatius showed the governor a letter written by the same Michael, in which he commended Ignatius very highly. The governor examined Michael, and the result was that he was exiled from Rome. After him followed Mindarra and Berrera, who said that Ignatius and his companions were fugitives from Spain, Paris, and Venice. Finally, however, in the presence of the governor and ambassador then at Rome, both acknowledged that they had nothing which they could say against them with regard to their doctrines or their lives. The ambassador ordered this lawsuit to be abandoned. Ignatius objected, saying that he wished the sentence to be made clear and public. This did not please the ambassador and the governor, nor even those who had previously taken sides with Ignatius. A few months afterward the Roman Pontiff returned. While he was at Tusculum Ignatius was admitted to an audience with the Holy Father, and having given some of his reasons, he obtained what he wished. The Pope ordered sentence to be passed, and it was given in favour of Ignatius and his companions.

Through the labours of Ignatius and his companions, certain pious works were established at Rome, as that of Catechumens, that of St Martha, and that of the Orphans. Master Natalis can tell the rest.

APPENDIX

ST. IGNATIUS AND HIS WORK FOR EDUCATION

In the kingdom of Navarre, in the north of Spain, among those mountains whence the armourers of Toledo drew their metal and forged for the world their trenchant steel, in a region where the generous, passionate, valiant people seemed to have formed their character on the austere grandeur of nature itself, St Ignatius was born.

The world represents him as a man of few and stern words, in appearance severe and dark, and yet a man in whom intellect is ever prominent, but intellect elevated by the grandeur of a soul of chivalry and by an exquisite delicacy of charity—this was the real character of St Ignatius. This will be seen in the brief glimpse given of his life and his spirit of charity, his absorbing love for souls, in his work of founding missions, his greatness of mind and heart, in the work originated by him, and carried on by his followers, in the cause of higher education.

His character stands prominently on the horizon of history. He cannot be ignored, nor is his existence or his work ignored.

His enemies have not passed him by without notice, and his friends, the friends of God, have rejoiced that, as God sent him forth to teach and produce fruit that the fruit might remain, the fruit has remained.

St Ignatius sends his voice down the centuries as a great individuality. He has spoken as a man of God, as a man of ideas, a man of energy. He has made his influence felt throughout the universe, not only in the civilized world, but in the uncivilized portion, to bring it into civilization, or to bear to it the advantages of civilization.

Other great men have spoken and have sent forth their influence. Theirs has been a message to the civilized world; it has been limited to one point of view. It has been prowess on the battlefield or on the seas, work in the ship of state or in the fields of science. But Ignatius has not been limited to any one of these. He is the founder of a Religious Order that has sent pioneers into all these fields and forests of valour or research; he is the writer of the Spiritual Exercises that have won a fame gained by but few authors; he is the father of many saints; he is the educator of generations; he is the inspirer of scientific, literary, theological, philosophical investigation, and the promoter of discoverers and of pioneer missionaries in the Old and the New World.

Ignatius was born, in 1491, at the château of Loyola, and at fifteen years of age he was a page in the court of King Ferdinand, and then a soldier under the Duke of Navarre, his relative. The army of Francis I penetrated into Navarre, and, at the siege of Pamplona, Ignatius, Captain of Infantry, was wounded by a cannon ball. His life is given in the preceding pages.

I shall refer only briefly to it, and to his conversion. He was a young knight fond of gaiety and feats of arms, and for some time after he received the wound he was confined to his bed while his broken leg was set; and while awaiting his slow recovery he read the lives of the saints and of Christ, as these were the books given to him in place of the novels he had asked for, as no others were in the house.

In reading the lives of the saints his heart was touched. His eyes were opened to the vanity of life and the reality of eternity compared with the worldliness of the life he had been leading. Inspired with enthusiasm at the lives of the saints, he said, 'What they have done, I can do.' The event of his life proved the earnestness of his purpose.

He resolved to undertake a life of penance and self-denial, and, while occupied with these holy resolutions, he wrote in a book the principal events of the life of Christ and His glorious Mother. It was at this time that Our Lord sent him a vision to strengthen and console him. He beheld one night, as he was holding his vigils, the glorious Queen of the angels, who appeared to him holding in her arms her Blessed Son, enlightening him with the splendour of glory and charming him by her sweet presence.

To her he ascribes the inspiration of the Spiritual Exercises, and his Order, imitating its founder, has shown the most unbounded affection and devoted filial love toward the Virgin Mother of Christ.

* * * * *

At Alcala St Ignatius studied, and there won for the Society of Jesus, Laynez, Salmeron, and Babadilla. He afterward founded there a college where Vasquez, Suarez, and St Francis Borgia expounded the Holy Scriptures. St Ignatius sent Father de Torres to Salamanca to found the famous college where the illustrious professors, Cardinal de Lugo, Francis Suarez, Maldonatus, Gregory of Valencia, Francis Ribera, and many other illustrious men were professors.

* * * * *

At the University of Paris, in 1534, on the 14th of March, St Ignatius received the degree of Master of Arts and Doctor of Philosophy, having received the degree of Bachelor of Arts two years before. The University of Paris had the honour of having as pupils St Ignatius, St Francis Xavier, Peter Faber, Claude le Jay, Simon Rodriguez, John Codura, Paschasius, Brouet, Martin Olave, all honoured with the academic degree.

* * * * *

Among the earlier colleges founded by St Ignatius were the following:—

In 1542 the College of Coimbra, in Portugal, arose. In 1546 St Francis Borgia founded the College of Gandia. In 1556 the College of Ingolstadt was founded. In 1552 a college was founded at Vienna, and in 1556 one at Prague. In 1553 the Roman College was fully founded. And in 1568 the colleges at Lima, Peru.

* * * * *

The German College founded in Rome by St Ignatius produced many remarkable men.

From it came 1 pope, Gregory XV, 24 cardinals, 6 electors of the Empire, 19 princes, 21 archbishops, 121 titular bishops, 100 bishops in *partibus infidelium*, 6 abbots or generals of religious orders, 11 martyrs of faith, 13 martyrs of charity, and 55 others, conspicuous for piety and learning.

This was at the end of the eighteenth century. In our own time in one classroom Father Cardella counted seventeen different orders of all different nationalities present at the lectures of theology in the Roman College.

* * * * *

The Roman College was the type of the Jesuit College. It was begun by Francis Borgia, in 1551, at the foot of the Capitol in Rome, with fourteen members of the Order and Father John Peltier, a Frenchman, as Superior.

The professors taught rhetoric and three languages,— Hebrew, Greek, and Latin. There were present there at a given time 2107 students, 300 in theology. The most eminent professors filled the chairs: theologians like Suarez and Vasquez; commentators such as Cornelius à Lapide and Maldonatus; founders of national history schools, as Mariana and Pallavicini; Clavius, reformer of the Gregorian Calendar; Kircher, universal in the exact sciences, while the other colleges throughout the world remained provided with their own required forces and maintained their own prestige.

*   *   *   *   *

From this college came forth distinguished men in every line of intellectual life, and general eminence, men of elevated thought and of noble and generous minds. In particular three characters came—young men that were to fill with admiration of their greatness the succeeding century.

Stanislaus Kostka, a Polish noble who died at seventeen years of age; Aloysius Gonzaga, an Italian prince of twenty-three; and John Berchmans, a Flemish townsman of twenty-two.

Among some of the famous men educated by the Jesuits we find Bossuet, Corneille, Molière, Tasso, Fontenelle, Diderot, Voltaire, and Bourdaloue, himself a Jesuit.

*   *   *   *   *

When Père Porée replied to the remark that he was not one of the great poets, he said, 'At least you may grant that I have been able to make some of them.' A few others were Descartes, Buffon, Justus Lipsius, Muratori the historian, Calderon, and Vico, the author of 'Ideas of History,' Richelieu, Tilly, Malesherbes, Don John of Austria, Luxembourg, Esterhazy, Choiseul, St Francis de Sales, Lambertini, afterward Benedict XIV, the most learned of the popes, and the present Pontiff, Pope Leo XIII, renowned for his learning and wisdom.

Nearly all the Jesuit writers had been Jesuit professors, with almost no exception, and nearly all had taught humanities, belles-lettres, and rhetoric. Father Southwell in 1676 numbers 2240 authors, and Father de Backer in 1876 counts 11,100.

AUTHORS

We find some remarkable authors among the Jesuit writers. Foremost come the Bollandists, renowned throughout the world for their monumental work, the 'Acta Sanctorum'. Similar gigantic works were carried on by Fathers de Backer, Sommervogel, and Pachtler. In the various branches of learning we need mention a few of the greater writers.

In astronomy, we find Ricci, Perry, De Vico, Secchi, Curley, Sestini.

In mathematics, Hagen, Algué.

In naval tactics, 'The Jesuit's Book.'

In archæology, Garucci, Marchi, the master of De Rossi.

In Oriental languages, Strassmaier, Harvas, Maas, Van den Gheyn.

In theology, Suarez, Vasquez, Toletus, Maldonatus, Franzelin.

In philosophy, Cominbricenses, Liberatore.

In moral philosophy, Busenbaum, Gury, Toledo, Ballerini, Layman, Lehmkuhl, Genicot.

In asceticism, Alvarez de Paz, Gaudier, Rodriguez, Scaramelli, Grou.

The Spiritual Exercises comprise a whole library. Father Watragan has written a work merely to record the editions and commentaries on these Exercises.

THE EDUCATIONAL PLAN OF ST. IGNATIUS

St Ignatius had gathered about him a body of picked men. The Roman College, the type of colleges of Jesuit education, would have for its professors only those who had been doctors of the University of Paris.

The outline of the course of education was given by St Ignatius. It was completed and developed by Aquaviva. The work was still more perfected by Father Laynez, of whom it is said,—

'St Ignatius praised him not only on account of other great merits, but particularly for devising and arranging the system of colleges.'

As to the number of students found under a unified method of thorough teaching, it will be interesting to take them in review.

In Rome in 1584, the twenty colleges attending classes in the Roman College numbered 2108 students, in Poland there were 10,000 young men chiefly of the nobility, at Rome 2000, at La Flèche 1700. In the seventeenth century at the College of Louis le Grand, in Paris, the number varied between 2000 and 3000. In 1627 the Province of Paris had in fourteen colleges 13,195 students.

The papal seminaries under Gregory XIII, at Vienna, Dillengen, Fulda, Prague, Grätz, Olmütz, Wilna, as well as in Japan, were directed by the Fathers, as also that of Pius V and of St Charles Borromeo at Milan.

Taking an average, there were more than two hundred thousand students being educated in these educational institutions.

A comparison could be made on this basis of the work done by the Order and that which is accomplished by Oxford.

If Oxford spends annually a revenue of $2,500,000 to supply facilities for higher education to two thousand of the nobility and gentry, how much would be required to educate a quarter of a million students,—not two thousand, but two hundred and fifty thousand?

The fundamental principles in the educational institute of St Ignatius were these:—

First, solidity and thoroughness.

The first condition of all higher studies as well as of lower studies was such that, as St Ignatius said, 'It was useless to begin at the top, as the edifice without a good foundation would never stand.'

Let literature and philosophy be gone through with satisfactorily, and then theology may be approached.

Literature must come first of all. St Ignatius provides for law and medicine, but by professors of law and medicine outside of the Order; but no professors of the Order were sent for work outside of Jesuit institutions. If the younger men were sent abroad, the younger generation would be deprived of that type; and if eminent men were sent forth without a permanent Jesuit College, the work would not be that of the Order, but of scattered individuals, and would soon perish.

In the cause of education St Ignatius had placed in his charter the watchwords 'Defence and Advance'. As a leader of a military type he had gathered about him the flower of youth and of mature age, from college and university, from doctor's chair and prince's throne, and in fifteen years from the foundation of the Order left one hundred colleges and houses in Portugal, Spain, Italy, Sicily, Germany, France, Brazil, and the East Indies. Xavier travelled from India and Ceylon, in the west, to Malucca, Japan, and the coast of China on the east. Wherever the energy and activity of Apostolic zeal penetrated it was with the purpose, and usually the result, of permanent Apostolic work in the foundation of educational institutions. Father de Backer says,—

'Wherever a Jesuit set his foot, wherever there was founded a house, a college, a mission, there too came apostles of another class, who laboured, who taught, who wrote.'

This is true even to our day where in the Rocky Mountains, beside the mission house of Spokane Falls, rises the Jesuit College of Spokane.

Sixty years later than the time of St Ignatius there were 272 colleges, and in 150 years the collegiate and university houses of education numbered 769.

'Looking at these seven hundred institutions of secondary and superior education,' says Father Thomas Hughes in his work on Loyola, 'in their scope of legislative executive power we find they were not so much a plurality of institutions as a single one.

'If we look at the 92 colleges in France, although the University of Paris was in one quarter of the city, and in that sense materially one,—although including 50 colleges,—yet in the formal and essential bond these 92 Jesuit colleges were vastly more of a unit as an identical educational power than any faculty existing. No faculty at Paris, Rome, Salamanca, or Oxford ever preserved the control over its 50, 20, or 8 colleges that each Provincial exercised over his 10, 20, or 30 colleges, or the general of the Order over the 700 colleges, with 22,126 members in the Order."

At the present day (1956) we find the Jesuit colleges in almost every part of the known world. In Rome and in China, in South Africa and North America, in the Philippine Islands as well as in Ceylon and Egypt, in Australia and Cuba, as well as in Syria and the city of New York.

We may glance briefly at the colleges scattered over the world, containing today 52,692 Jesuit pupils.

This is a larger number than those taught at Oxford and Cambridge and Glasgow and Harvard or Yale or Princeton or in Paris and Edinburgh.

There has been no going back. Fifty years ago, when the groundwork of rebuilding the 700 institutions that had been destroyed by the suppression had to be commenced all over again, there were but 15,000, today there are 52,692.

St Ignatius was born in 1491. The first College of Coimbra was founded in 1542. From 1542 to 1773 is a period of 231 years. The suppression lasted from 1773 to 1814 (41 years). The new work continued from 1814 to 1899, a period of 85 years.

Among the colleges founded in the chief cities of the world are Loyola College, at Loyola in Spain; St Omer's

College, in Belgium, the link between Europe and America; Stonyhurst College, in England; Clongoes Wood, Ireland; Mangalore, in India, the only first-grade college in the district; Melbourne, Australia; St Ignatius College, California, the pioneer of Pacific coast missions and of the Rocky Mountains; at Kansas City the only boarding college in the far West; St Ignatius, at Cleveland, Ohio, one of the latest Western colleges; Spring Hill College, at Mobile, Alabama; Georgetown College, at Washington, D.C.; Holy Cross College, at Worcester, Massachusetts; St John's College, at Fordham, New York; St Francis Xavier's College, in New York City.

In the proportion mentioned above, in the same period (that is, a period of 231 years), there will be in the Jesuit colleges 263,690 pupils.

St Ignatius died July 31, 1556. He was sixty-five years of age. At the age of thirty he hung up his sword at Montserrat, and, with ready mind and heart and pen, in thirty-five years he achieved the gigantic work of the founding and developing the Order. The educational work was projected and advanced in a brief period of fifteen years, from 1542 to 1556.

He was a man of prudence and deliberation, and of unswerving decision.

Vigilant and patient, whenever he appeared account had to be taken of the man; and so with his Order, whenever it appears it is to be recognised either by foes to oppose it or friends to love it and forward its work. It has its churches—its missions—its colleges. In its churches it is faithful to the teaching of Christ and His Church, loyal ever to the Vicar of Christ; in its missions, unbounded in zeal and personal self-sacrifice; in its colleges, it aims ever at the solid and thorough training of complete Christian education. Ignatius of Loyola made his Order to go on without him, and it goes on just as he made it.

www.ingramcontent.com/pod-product-compliance
Lightning Source LLC
Chambersburg PA
CBHW031428290426
44110CB00011B/573

9780975658888